W9-ACU-795

# Training Managers to Train

*Developing Diverse Talents*

## Third Edition

# Brother Herman E. Zaccarelli, C.S.C.

## *A Crisp Fifty-Minute™ Series Book*

This Fifty-Minute™ book is designed to be "read with a pencil." It is an excellent workbook for self-study as well as classroom learning. All material is copyright-protected and cannot be duplicated without permission from the publisher. *Therefore, be sure to order a copy for every training participant by contacting:*

## THOMSON
### ★
### COURSE TECHNOLOGY™

1-800-442-7477 • 25 Thomson Place, Boston MA • www.courseilt.com

# Training Managers to Train

*Developing Diverse Talents*

Third Edition

**Brother Herman E. Zaccarelli, C.S.C.**

## CREDITS:
Senior Editor: **Debbie Woodbury**
Editor: **Ann Gosch**
Assistant Editor: **Genevieve McDermott**
Production Manager: **Denise Powers**
Design: **Nicole Phillips**
Production Artist: **Rich Lehl**
Cartoonist: **Ralph Mapson**

For more information contact:

Course Technology
25 Thomson Place
Boston, MA 02210

Or find us on the Web at **www.courseilt.com**

For permission to use material from this text or product, submit a request online at www.thomsonrights.com.

**Trademarks**
Crisp Fifty-Minute Series is a trademark of Course Technology. Some of the product names and company names used in this book have been used for identification purposes only, and may be trademarks or registered trademarks of their respective manufacturers and sellers.

**Disclaimer**
Course Technology reserves the right to revise this publication and make changes from time to time in its content without notice.

**ISBN** 1-56052-700-5
Library of Congress Catalog Card Number 2003098908
Printed in Canada by Webcom Limited

4 5 6 PM 06 05 04

# Learning Objectives For:

## TRAINING MANAGERS TO TRAIN

The objectives for *Training Managers to Train, Third Edition* are listed below. They have been developed to guide you, the reader, to the core issues covered in this book.

### THE OBJECTIVES OF THIS BOOK ARE:

❑ 1) To explain why managers should learn to train

❑ 2) To explore key concepts in training adults in the workplace

❑ 3) To show the role of position analysis in defining a training program

❑ 4) To present practical methods for planning and implementing on-the-job training (OJT)

❑ 5) To present guidelines for evaluating the effectiveness of a manager's training efforts

### ASSESSING YOUR PROGRESS

In addition to the learning objectives above, Course Technology has developed a Crisp Series **assessment** that covers the fundamental information presented in this book. A 25-item, multiple-choice and true/false questionnaire allows the reader to evaluate his or her comprehension of the subject matter. To buy the assessment and answer key, go to www.courseilt.com and search on the book title or via the assessment format, or call 1-800-442-7477.

*Assessments should not be used in any employee selection process.*

# About the Author

Brother Herman E. Zaccarelli, C.S.C., is presently the Director of Special Projects at Stonehill College in Easton, Massacusetts. Previously, he was the Director of the Educational Conference Center at Kings College in Pennsylvania. Brother Herman has also served as Director of the Restaurant and Hotel Management Institute at Purdue University.

Brother Herman received his Master of Science in Business Administration from St. Thomas University, Miami, Florida. A prolific writer, he has published more than 100 articles in professional magazines and is the author of a dozen books. He has been the recipient of numerous business and industry awards.

## *How to Use This Book*

This *Fifty-Minute™ Series Book* is a unique, user-friendly product. As you read through the material, you will quickly experience the interactive nature of the book. There are numerous exercises, real-world case studies, and examples that invite your opinion, as well as checklists, tips, and concise summaries that reinforce your understanding of the concepts presented.

A Crisp Learning *Fifty-Minute™ Book* can be used in a variety of ways. Individual self-study is one of the most common. However, many organizations use *Fifty-Minute* books for pre-study before a classroom training session. Other organizations use the books as a part of a systemwide learning program—supported by video and other media based on the content in the books. Still others work with Crisp Learning to customize the material to meet their specific needs and reflect their culture. Regardless of how it is used, we hope you will join the more than 20 million satisfied learners worldwide who have completed a *Fifty-Minute Book*.

# *Dedication*

In his book, *The Clowns of God,* author Morris West writes, "We are met most powerfully at the crossroads. We'll part each richer."

I was at the crossroads in the eighth grade, 59 years ago.

It was the crossroads of adolescence, with all that the word implies. My eighth grade teacher, Sister Paul Marie Sohl, was a nun who was years ahead of her time in educational psychology. She had a special gift of helping her students reach their potential. Sister Paul Marie empowered us through her encouragement to believe that we could be anything we wanted to be. The students always meant so much more to her than simply their IQ level.

During the past 65 years, Sister Paul Marie has made an extraordinary contribution to Catholic education in the United States as a teacher and administrator, and as a consultant to Catholic education. To all these ministries of service she brought exceptional energy, creativity, and collaborative management. Her faith and love for the church, which she has served for over 70 years, is a play that Shakespeare could never write; a poem Robert Frost could not pen.

I dedicate this book to Sister Paul Marie Sohl, a great woman of the church who first inspired me 59 years ago to believe that I could be anything I wanted to be, with a deep spirit of faith in God and a desire to serve humankind.


Brother Herman Zaccarelli

# Preface

Management has been described as the process of achieving goals by coordinating the efforts of a group. Managers at all organizational levels, whether they own their own business or work for someone else, must supervise people. Done correctly, everyone benefits and the manager receives credit for a job well done. If, on the other hand, employees are not managed effectively, goals may not be achieved, and the manager will quickly get the blame!

At all organizational levels, most employees want to do a good job at work. But employees cannot perform well on the job no matter how hard they try and no matter how much they want to until they know what they are supposed to do and how they are supposed to do it.

In some large organizations, professional trainers are responsible for letting workers know what is expected of them. In many organizations, however, the task of explaining to and showing workers what they need to know is the job of their managers. Of course, managers must accomplish this task in addition to all of their other, non-training-related tasks. As a result, some managers do not adequately train. When that happens, the manager, the workers, and the organization itself may all suffer.

*Training Managers to Train, Third Edition* focuses on answering the question: How does a manager plan, implement, and evaluate training programs designed to help employees with diverse backgrounds, skills, and experience become better at their jobs and, as a result, meet the organization's goals?

The answer to this question is presented in the pages that follow. Professional trainers know the key principles and practices for successful training development and delivery. These are shared in this edition and labeled as "Professional Trainer's Tip." Watch for these special boxes.

Training programs can be fun to develop and to implement. And they can make a significant difference in your organization's success. Readers will find this book easy to read and use. The effort spent learning about training by putting this book's basic principles to work can be rewarding to everyone—management, employees, and customers.

We're excited to bring this material to you. We hope you enjoy using it.

# Contents

## Part 4: Plan the Training

## Part 5: Present the Training

## Part 6: Evaluate the Training

# Appendix

# Training Responsibility Survey

Before you begin, take a few minutes to think about the training process and how it affects your own job. Evaluate your present responsibility for training and check (✔) the statements below that are true for you. The more checkmarks you have, the more important it is for you to become a competent "manager/trainer."

I am:

❑ Responsible for the quality of my group's work.

❑ Responsible for the quantity of work my group produces.

❑ Sometimes required to implement changes in how we perform our work.

❑ Primarily responsible for getting new workers "up to speed" in my area.

❑ In a job where my work group experiences regular turnover.

❑ Currently working with a diverse group of employees.

❑ Responsible for deciding which current staff members will help show new staff what to do.

❑ Often called upon to teach employees one-on-one.

❑ Sometimes responsible for group training.

❑ Regularly called upon to explain the productivity of my work group to upper management.

❑ Required to recruit new employees.

❑ Required to schedule new employees.

❑ Evaluated, to some degree, on my ability to train employees properly.

❑ Responsible for training all new employees in my work group.

❑ Interested in learning more about training as part of my regular management responsibilities.

# The Case for Manager-Led Training

2

# Training Benefits the Organization

Training can provide innumerable benefits. You, your customers, your employees, and your organization have much to gain—and nothing to lose—with a high-quality training program.

Which of the following benefits will your organization receive if the work group for which you are responsible is well trained?

❑ **Saving money:** If employees know how to do the work the right way with fewer errors, costs will be lower and profits will be higher.

❑ **Saving employees:** Employees who know how to do the work according to their manager's expectations will be less anxious and turnover will be reduced.

❑ **Saving customers and making new ones:** Customers are happy when they receive the products and services they expect. Training helps ensure that this will consistently happen.

❑ **Saving time:** A trained staff will promote efficiency. Both the manager's time and that of employees will be saved because the work is completed properly the first time.

❑ **Reducing staffing concerns:** Trained employees are better prepared and more eligible for promotion opportunities.

❑ **Saving relationships:** Managers who show their concern for employees with quality training help motivate them, and morale levels are likely to increase.

❑ **Increased management flexibility:** Well-trained employees allow managers greater flexibility when scheduling because larger numbers of workers have acquired the skills needed to meet the organization's goals.

❑ **Improving managers' skills:** Managers who learn to train understand their employees' tasks better than managers who do not train. The result is a greater appreciation of employees' needs, problems, and concerns.

You should have checked all the boxes because all of these represent benefits any organization will receive from its employees being well trained.

# Training Benefits Employees

Employees always benefit from training. An important part of a manager's job is to demonstrate how training will help employees. In most cases, employees will want to be trained because they, as well as the organization, will benefit from their training experience.

**Trainees who understand the benefits they will receive from training**

**Managers who take their training responsibilities seriously**

**Training success!**

Check (✔) any of the following you would like your employees to achieve:

☐ Personal knowledge that the job was done well

☐ Promotion

☐ Freedom from on-the-job accidents

☐ Wage or salary increase

☐ Anxiety-free performance evaluations

☐ Increase in tips (where applicable)

☐ Fewer customer complaints

☐ Freedom from on-the-job boredom

☐ Less tiresome work

☐ Feeling of being a "professional"

☐ Participation in career development programs

☐ Respect and esteem from customers, peers, and managers

☐ Good first on-the-job experiences

☐ Knowledge of job security

☐ Less stress

☐ Improved teamwork

☐ Better relationship with your manager

☐ More fun on the job

☐ Job enjoyment

You may have checked all of the factors. Each is influenced by training.

## Professional Trainer's Tip

Always make sure you understand and can communicate to your trainees how they will benefit from the training they will receive. Let the trainees know the benefit(s) early in the training process because it will help motivate them to learn.

# Training New Employees

Some managers believe they do not need to train new employees because these employees are already experienced when they are hired. Yet although employees may be hired with specific work skills, there is still much they must be taught.

Using the following checklist, identify those items that new employees would need to be informed about to be comfortable in their new jobs.

❑ Appearance and dress

❑ Attendance

❑ Bulletin boards

❑ Company publications

❑ Dental insurance

❑ Departmental meetings

❑ Disciplinary system

❑ Educational assistance

❑ Emergency procedures

❑ E-mail policy

❑ Employee opinion survey

❑ Employee recognition

❑ General meetings

❑ Grievance procedures

❑ Health, safety, and accident policies

❑ Holidays

❑ Insurance policies and benefits

❑ Jury duty policies

❑ Layoff policy

❑ Leaves of absence

❑ Lost articles

❑ Meals

❑ Name badges

❑ Overtime

❑ Parking

❑ Pay advances

❑ Pay discrepancies and adjustments

❑ Pay policy

❑ Pay periods and paydays

❑ Performance appraisals

❑ Personal property

❑ Probationary period

❑ Public transportation

❑ Recreational and social activities

❑ Retirement program

❑ Seniority

❑ Service award banquet

❑ Sick leave

❑ Sign-in/Sign-out sheets

❑ Standards of conduct

❑ Telephone calls

❑ Time records

❑ Tips

❑ Training procedures

❑ Uniforms

❑ Vacations

❑ Wage and salary reviews

❑ Work schedules

❑ Other _____

In your organization, whose job is it to teach new employees about these things?

_____

Whose job is it to explain these items further if the employee is confused ?

_____

# Training Is Part of Effective Supervision

A manager must do many things at once. All are important. And for most managers, training should be one of the most important, highest-priority activities they do. The best managers take time to train.

Training is essential to the development of staff members. Just as a well-coached team performs better than a poorly coached one, so too a well-trained workforce performs better than a poorly trained one.

To be an effective supervisor, you cannot think of training as "nice to do," but rather as a "must do." Good training results in clear, measurable improvements in individual and group performance. And better performance by employees means better performance for the organization as a whole.

This is why training must receive a high priority from upper management. The highest levels of management must agree about the importance of training and allocate time and resources for it to be done well.

If you have been assigned the responsibility for training but do not have all the time or resources needed to implement the training, ask your own manager for help.

# Managers Routinely Face Situations Requiring Training

Some organizations have full-time trainers, but even then, situations arise that require managers who are *not* full-time trainers to be responsible for some training even as they continue to perform their regular jobs.

As a manager, you may have faced, or will face, some of these situations. When you do, you must have mastered the skills and techniques required to provide outstanding training.

Under which of the following conditions do you think your organization (and your employees) would count on you to use your training skills? Circle the numbers for all that apply.

1. New workers must be oriented and educated in policies, procedures, and standards.

2. Changes in product and service offerings mean employees must acquire new skills.

3. Changes in processes and procedures require employees to acquire new skills.

4. An absence, or temporary shortage, of full-time trainers requires that managers assume the trainer's role.

5. Problems in production quality require increased training.

6. Problems in production quantity require increased training.

7. The organization implements new policies or procedures.

8. Managers must pass on to the employees knowledge and skills that only the managers know.

9. Managers must prepare employees for new jobs so the organization can continue to grow.

10. Managers must prepare their own replacements to take over their jobs when they are promoted or transferred.

# The Ability to Train Makes a Better Manager

**Good managers are able to:**

- ☑ Plan
- ☑ Organize
- ☑ Staff
- ☑ Supervise
- ☑ Coordinate
- ☑ Control
- ☑ Evaluate

**Managers must manage:**

- ☑ Time
- ☑ People (Employees)
- ☑ Money
- ☑ Materials
- ☑ Energy
- ☑ Procedures
- ☑ Equipment

As managers supervise employees, they must:

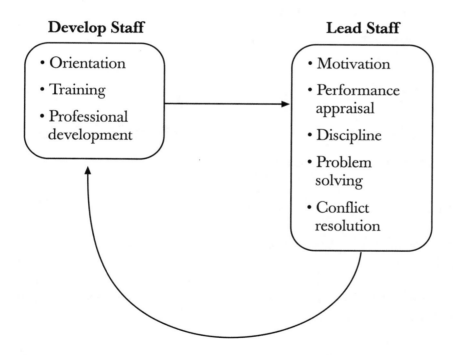

**Develop Staff**

- Orientation
- Training
- Professional development

**Lead Staff**

- Motivation
- Performance appraisal
- Discipline
- Problem solving
- Conflict resolution

In most cases, staff must be trained *before* they can be led. When managers develop the ability to train employees effectively in addition to their other skills, they become even more valuable to their organizations. In today's globally competitive workplace, good managers who are also good trainers are in high demand.

# Managers Often Make the Best Trainers

Managers who train their employees face different challenges than do professional, full-time trainers. For most managers, the majority of training they conduct is on-the-job training (OJT). That is, the training takes place while the employee is on the job working, rather than sitting in a "classroom." Managers often know the best way to teach the "tricks of the trade." They simply know more about the job at hand.

Think about your own job knowledge. In your area of responsibility, do you know:

|  | Yes | No |
|---|---|---|
| The quality and quantity standards that are in place? | ❑ | ❑ |
| How best to do the job? | ❑ | ❑ |
| Where the job is best completed? | ❑ | ❑ |
| What obstacles to success may be present? | ❑ | ❑ |
| How to avoid those obstacles? | ❑ | ❑ |
| How long the job should take? | ❑ | ❑ |
| When it is the busiest? | ❑ | ❑ |
| How employees should use their time when the business is not busy? | ❑ | ❑ |
| Work shortcuts that still allow employees to maintain quality? | ❑ | ❑ |
| Where employees should go for help when needed? | ❑ | ❑ |

Besides possessing superior job knowledge, managers are most likely in the best position to tell employees why the specific training being provided is important and how it will make the job better and more interesting. The best managers find that OJT is an important part of nearly every employee's professional development, and they want to do it well.

## Professional Trainer's Tip

The best trainers do not imply that they "know it all." If trainees ask questions for which you do not know the answer, let the trainees know you will find the answer and get back to them. They will respect your honesty and you will learn something new too.

# Where Training and Learning Meet

# Making Change Happen

By now you have learned that your job as a manager is to train your employees. Your employee's job is to learn. What is learning? Very simply, learning is change. Training is how you make learning, and change, happen.

Think about the last new skill you learned and write it here:

_____

Now answer the following questions:

1. Did someone help you learn?

_____

2. How did the person help?

_____

3. How long did it take you to catch on?

_____

4. Was the result worth the time invested?

_____

5. In what way(s)?

_____

_____

There is an old saying that if a trainee has not learned, it is because the trainer has not trained. In most cases, the manager *shares* responsibility with the trainees for learning what must be learned.

## Professional Trainer's Tip

Remember that trainees will learn at different rates of speed. That is normal. Do not expect all your trainees to catch on as quickly as the fastest learners. Sometimes the fast-learning trainees can help you teach other trainees who are having a more difficult time.

# Workplace Change and the Ongoing Need for Training

It has often been said that change is the only constant in life. That is certainly true in many organizations. Today's workplace is, in most cases, very different from how it was only a few years ago.

Because the workplace changes so rapidly, you may be assigned the responsibility of helping your work group adapt and learn new and better ways of doing things. You know that part of your job as a manager is to help your employees learn the new things they need to know to be successful.

But change can be scary. Assume that you are a worker facing a major change in how you will do your job. Assume also that your manager will help you, through training, to master the new things you must know. Which of the following emotions would you likely feel?

| | | |
|---|---|---|
| ❏ Apprehensive | ❏ Glad | ❏ Pleased |
| ❏ Uncomfortable | ❏ Hopeful | ❏ Challenged |
| ❏ Overwhelmed | ❏ Cautious | ❏ Self-doubting |
| ❏ Excited | ❏ Worried | ❏ Nervous |
| ❏ Concerned | ❏ Angry | ❏ Unsure |

People often get comfortable with the familiar ways of "doing" and "thinking." But today's world changes too fast for that kind of behavior. To help your employees learn to readily accept change and the new things they will need to learn, try the following tips:

| When Your Employees: | You Can: |
|---|---|
| Say they don't know how | Tell them you will teach them |
| Claim they can't | Show them how they can |
| Get frustrated | Give them more practice time |
| Want to give up | Keep encouraging them |
| Learn the new way | Tell them you are proud of their success |

# Three Keys to Adult Learning

If you are a manager assigned to train your staff, you will likely be teaching adults while they are working. In most cases, adults approach learning differently than youngsters do.

Children really like to learn new things. Adults, on the other hand, are more complex. To teach adults in the most effective way, be sure that they:

➤ **Want to learn**–Tell your employees exactly what benefits they will get out of the training process.

➤ **Have time to learn**–Plan the training to take place over a reasonable period of time.

➤ **Have a chance to practice**–Effective training is more than just "telling." It also gives trainees a chance to try out the new information or skill in a realistic setting.

## Professional Trainer's Tip

Do not try to teach too much–create too much change–at one time. Remember that several training sessions with smaller amounts of new information will nearly always produce better results than will one long training session.

# Training at the Intersection of Attitude and Knowledge

Done effectively, training is good for everyone—the manager, employees, and the customers. But will training solve all the problems of the business? Will all situations be improved by training? The answer to both questions is no. Training works best for employees who are interested in learning the knowledge and skills required to do the job.

To analyze training's potential effectiveness, it helps to analyze affected employees' perceived attitude (good or poor) and their level of job knowledge (high or low).

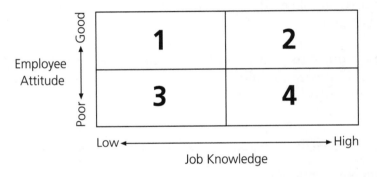

Let's look at the possibilities where the two traits (attitude and knowledge) come together:

**BOX 1**    (Good Attitude/Low Job Knowledge)—An employee with a good attitude and low level of job knowledge can be helped dramatically by training.

**BOX 2**    (Good Attitude/High Job Knowledge)—Training will help this employee, providing there are adequate time, resources, and so on.

**BOX 3**    (Poor Attitude/Low Job Knowledge)—Personnel action (such as reassigning duties) may be most appropriate in this situation. Training is unlikely to help if the person who needs training is not interested in learning.

**BOX 4**    (Poor Attitude/High Job Knowledge)—This employee could do the job with the proper attitude; but without it, training will not reduce the problem.

Training works when the employee wants to learn (has a positive attitude) but does not know how to do the required work.

# Allowing for Varied Learning Preferences

Just as every person is an individual, every person has his or her own learning style. It is usually not possible, of course, to develop a separate training program for each individual employee. But neither should you ignore the varied learning preferences of those you are training.

The following lists will help you take into account the many learning preferences in tools, atmosphere, format, and leader. Circle the items that reflect your own learning preferences.

**Learning Tools**
Books
Workbooks
Audiotapes
Videotapes
Computer-based

**Learning Formats**
On-the-job training
One-on-one teaching
Small group study
Large group presentation
Self-study

**Learning Atmosphere**
Indoors
Outdoors
Quiet
Background music
Noisy discussion

**Learning Leader**
Outside "expert"
Professional instructor
Boss
Co-worker
Self-directed

## Professional Trainer's Tip

Consider the backgrounds and educational levels of your trainees before you choose learning tools. Those trainees with limited reading skills, for example, would not do well in a reading-intensive training structure.

# Respecting Diversity in the Workplace

Most workplaces today are very different from how they were only a few years ago. So, too, are the people who make up today's workforce. Everyone brings his or her own unique personality traits to training.

The employees you will train are young adults and old. They may come from a variety of backgrounds and cultures. They are both experienced and newly hired. And they may be concerned about their ability to "learn" what you will teach them.

Despite differences among themselves, they share the need to be well trained. As a manager-trainer, your job, in part, is to train all of your employees in a manner that recognizes their individual worth and value to your organization.

When managers who will be doing training recognize and respond to these individual differences and training needs, the manager, the workers, and the organization for which they work all benefit.

Think about the work group you are responsible for training. In the following diversity checklist, place a check (✔) in the boxes of the areas in which your group varies.

## Diversity Checklist:

❏ Age

❏ Ambitions

❏ Education

❏ Ethnicity

❏ Experience

❏ Gender

❏ Geographic origin

❏ Income

❏ Interests

❏ Job status

❏ Literacy

❏ Marital status

❏ Parental status

❏ Personality

❏ Physical ability

❏ Primary language

❏ Race

❏ Religion

❏ Sexual orientation

❏ Wellness

Which, if any, of these differences do you think will affect how your group adapts to change and learning?

_____

_____

_____

How?

_____

_____

_____

## Professional Trainer's Tip

Spend time considering the specific makeup of your trainee group. The more you understand about how they learn, the more effective your training sessions will become.

# The Four Steps of Training

This part of the book has explained several factors that must come together for your training to result in employee learning. Now that you understand the keys to adult learning, the remainder of this guide will present the four steps of training. The basic procedures for effective training, regardless of the depth of the training, involve the following four-step method:

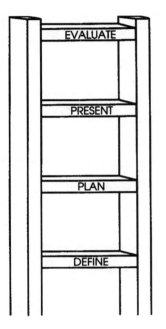

**Step #4:** Evaluate the Training

**Step #3:** Present the Training

**Step #2:** Plan the Training

**Step #1:** Define How the Job Should Be Done

## *Using the Four-Step Method*

Once you have mastered these basic four steps, you can use them any time you implement training activities. These basics should be used consistently whether you are:

➤ Training and orienting new employees

➤ Upgrading the knowledge and skills of existing staff

➤ Providing long-term professional development

➤ Resolving operating problems or improving operating efficiency

### Professional Trainer's Tip

Poorly planned training will generally yield poor results. The best trainers carefully consider their trainees and their needs, and then they follow *each* of the four training steps every time a new training program is implemented. Employees should not be trained to do a job until the correct way to do the work has been *defined*. But this first step is too often omitted.

As you work through this book, you will learn how to define jobs and acquire the knowledge and skills necessary to be a good trainer.

# TAKE THE TRAINING TEST

Which of the following statements about training are true, false, or partially true (maybe)? Place a check (✔) in the appropriate column to indicate your answers.

|  | True | False | Maybe |
|---|:---:|:---:|:---:|
| 1. Training can be difficult. | ❏ | ❏ | ❏ |
| 2. Training should be cost-effective. | ❏ | ❏ | ❏ |
| 3. Training is a line responsibility. | ❏ | ❏ | ❏ |
| 4. Only new employees benefit from training. | ❏ | ❏ | ❏ |
| 5. Training can modify an employee's attitudes. | ❏ | ❏ | ❏ |
| 6. Training is best when objectives involve increasing or changing knowledge or skill levels. | ❏ | ❏ | ❏ |
| 7. Training should be done when time permits. | ❏ | ❏ | ❏ |
| 8. Training for problem resolution is different from teaching job skills to a new employee. | ❏ | ❏ | ❏ |

*Compare your answers to the author's responses in the Appendix.*

# Define How the Job Should Be Done

24

# Developing a Position Analysis

A trainer must know how a job should be done before the "best" way to do that job can be taught. Quality standards can be defined, time and cost requirements can be established, and guidelines for performance evaluation criteria can be developed only when employees perform job tasks consistently.

This is why the first step in training is *defining* how the job should be done. This requires what is called a *position analysis,* which involves the following four activities:

1. Develop a list of tasks

2. Define each task

3. Determine required quality levels

4. Construct a job description

In this section, you will learn a process for position analysis that is simple, practical, and efficient.

## SEEKING CONSISTENCY

How consistently do employees in your organization perform their jobs? Check (✔) each of the following statements true or false as they apply to your organization.

|  | True | False |
|---|:---:|:---:|
| 1. All employees in the same position perform each of their job tasks in the same way. | ❑ | ❑ |
| 2. Every supervisor for a specific area of responsibility would give the same explanation of how each task should be done. | ❑ | ❑ |
| 3. Different employees take about the same amount of time to perform the same, specific task. | ❑ | ❑ |
| 4. All employees use the same process or procedures to perform identical tasks. | ❑ | ❑ |
| 5. Customers compliment your organization about the consistency of employee task procedures they encounter. | ❑ | ❑ |
| 6. Similar quality standards are consistently attained by all employees. | ❑ | ❑ |
| 7. The definition of what constitutes "good" performance is understood by all members of the staff and is used as the basis for training, supervision, and performance appraisals. | ❑ | ❑ |
| 8. Job descriptions accurately portray the work to be done. | ❑ | ❑ |

If you answered candidly, you probably answered many or all of the above statements false. If you think about each question, however, you probably realize that in an ideal organization, most questions would be answered true. This is where the position analysis comes in. It fosters consistency in job performance by defining how jobs should be done.

# Activity #1: Develop a List of Tasks

**Position Analysis:**
**The Four Activities**

❑ Develop a list of tasks

❑ Define each task

❑ Determine required quality levels

❑ Design a job description

The first activity in analyzing any position is developing a task list. This list will specify all job elements that an employee (such as a sales clerk, computer operator, or maintenance supervisor) must do to satisfy that position's job requirements. Once a manager/trainer identifies and lists these activities, the training program can be defined.

How is a task list developed?

1. Think about the required tasks to perform a specific job.

2. Observe employees in that job and what they do.

3. Discuss with employees the tasks they do and ask which are the most important and why.

4. Ask other supervisors to identify tasks that their team members perform in similar job situations.

5. Study the job description to see how accurately it reflects the specific job's objectives.

# SAMPLE TASK LIST

Position:_____

Specific tasks required to perform in this position, listed by priority:

1. _____

2. _____

3. _____

4. _____

5. _____

List all significant tasks that an employee working in a specific position must do. For example, a sales clerk, as part of the job, may:

➤ Operate the cash register correctly for each transaction (daily)

➤ Complete a daily sales report to the specifications required (daily)

➤ Attend to customers (daily)

➤ Conduct inventory counts (weekly)

➤ Vacuum the carpet (daily)

Once all basic tasks have been identified, a manager with training responsibilities will know what a new sales clerk must accomplish.

To be successful, a training program must present all of the necessary information to allow a newly hired sales clerk to understand and perform the job to the quality level expected.

For more practice in developing task lists, turn to the practice activity in the Appendix.

# Activity #2: Define Each Task

| Position Analysis: The Four Activities |
|---|
| ❑ Develop a list of tasks |
| ❑ Define each task |
| ❑ Determine required quality levels |
| ❑ Design a job description |

The second activity for position analysis is breaking down each task into smaller tasks. This breakdown answers the question, "How exactly should a task be performed?" It should tell the "how, when, and what" of each task and specify any required equipment, supplies, or procedures needed.

How is a task breakdown developed? You can apply the same process used to develop a task list.

1. Think about the preferred way for employees to perform a task.

2. Observe and consult employees who do the work.

3. Ask supervisors of those who do similar tasks to explain the ideal way to complete each task.

**Note:** A careful analysis of how work is currently done will likely yield excellent ideas about how it can be improved. Although a "new way" is not always better, often there are better ways to accomplish any task.

# SAMPLE TASK BREAKDOWN

Position _____  Task _____

**The procedures to complete this task include:**

| Step | Process | Equipment/ Supplies | Time Requirements | Other |
|------|---------|---------------------|-------------------|-------|
| 1. |  |  |  |  |
| 2. |  |  |  |  |
| 3. |  |  |  |  |
| 4. |  |  |  |  |
| 5. |  |  |  |  |

A task breakdown describes, in sequence, what employees must do to perform a task correctly. Consider, for example, a sales clerk operating a cash register. Operating instructions provided by the equipment manufacturer might be an excellent starting point. These can then be integrated into the specific job requirements.

But the answers to other questions—such as "How exactly should inventory counts be taken?" or "What considerations are necessary when approaching a customer?"—cannot be supplied in a manufacturer's instruction booklet. The procedures that evolve to answer questions such as these can be beneficial even before training activities begin.

_____

For more practice in developing task breakdowns, turn to the practice activity in the Appendix.

# Activity #3: Determine Required Quality Levels

> **Position Analysis:**
> **The Four Activities**
>
> ❑ Develop a list of tasks
>
> ❑ Define each task
>
> ❑ Determine required quality levels
>
> ❑ Design a job description

The third activity in analyzing a position is determining the quality level required for the task. What must be done to ensure these quality standards are met? This is the question this activity addresses.

Today everyone is talking about the need for improved quality. Studies show that customers are willing to pay extra for quality service. And businesses lose customers when quality is lacking. Customers have long memories when quality problems occur.

Managers must design quality standards into the way work is done. Training programs by managers must stress quality and, more important, must show each employee why quality is essential.

Trainers must:

➤ Ensure that the task breakdown will yield output that meets or exceeds quality standards.

➤ Constantly stress quality as an integral part of each task.

➤ Show how quality standards are built into work output.

➤ Identify those products or services that do not meet quality standards and correct them.

**Note:** Trainees may not be able to attain required quality levels immediately. They need time to build the skills necessary to meet quality standards. By the time training is completed, however, trainees should be able to identify quality requirements and understand the target date for meeting the desired quality levels.

# Quality Standards Test

Check (✔) the following statements that are true in your organization:

❏ Quality standards have been established for all activities undertaken by persons in all positions.

❏ Quality of work output is a significant factor in employee appraisals.

❏ Customer complaints about quality problems are extremely rare.

❏ Quality is just as important as quantity when tasks are performed.

❏ Quality standards are consistently measured and reported on.

❏ Management's philosophy and expectations about maintaining quality standards are well known.

❏ Employee training programs emphasize quality requirements as skills that are taught.

❏ Employees are rewarded by meeting (or exceeding) quality goals.

How many did you check as true? Any that were not checked need immediate action.

Think about the products and services you purchase as a consumer and answer the following questions:

What makes you happy? Disappointed?

_____

What quality factors apply to the products or services that your organization provides?

_____

What can you learn from this analysis?

_____

How can you apply your own perceptions of quality to the way things are done by your employees?

_____

## Professional Trainer's Tip

Most skills are difficult before they become easy. This is true when producing quality products or providing quality service. Make sure trainees have plenty of practice time and that they do not become discouraged if they do not produce excellent results the first time they try.

# Activity #4: Design a Job Description

> ### Position Analysis:
> ### The Four Activities
>
> ❏ Develop a list of tasks
>
> ❏ Define each task
>
> ❏ Determine required quality levels
>
> ❏ Design a job description

The final activity in position analysis is designing a job description. This important human resources management tool has many uses. A trainer with a current job description has a head start in ensuring that employees recruited and selected have the "right" training activities.

**Note:** Large organizations typically have human resources departments to help recruit employees. It is important that operating departments provide the HR department with updated job descriptions. If this does not occur, there may be "surprises" when a newly hired employee "discovers" what the job really involves.

# SAMPLE JOB DESCRIPTION*

Position:_____ Date of Last Revision: ___/___/___

Level:_____

1) This position reports to:_____

2) This position supervises: _____

3) Basic tasks for this position include: _____

    A)_____
    B) _____
    C)_____
    D)_____
    E) _____
    F) _____
    G)_____
    H)_____

4) Knowledge of equipment required includes:

_____

5) Personal qualifications judged most important for this job are:

_____

6) Quality standards for this position ensure:

_____

7) Other important aspects of this position are:

_____

8) Other:

_____

➤   Only the most important tasks should be included in the job description.

➤   "Personal qualities" are sometimes included in a separate "job specifications" sheet. In the sample description above, they are combined.

*Note: This is a simplified version of a job description.

# Uses for a Job Description

Once developed, a job description can be used for many purposes. It is as useful when recruiting applicants as for guiding employees after they have been hired. Included among the uses for a job description are the following:

➤ To inform applicants being recruited about important aspects of the job

➤ To indicate the job requirements to be addressed during training

➤ As a management tool to help supervise employees

➤ To assist in employee appraisal (employees should be evaluated on how well they do the work specified in the job description)

➤ As an aid in developing compensation rates for different positions

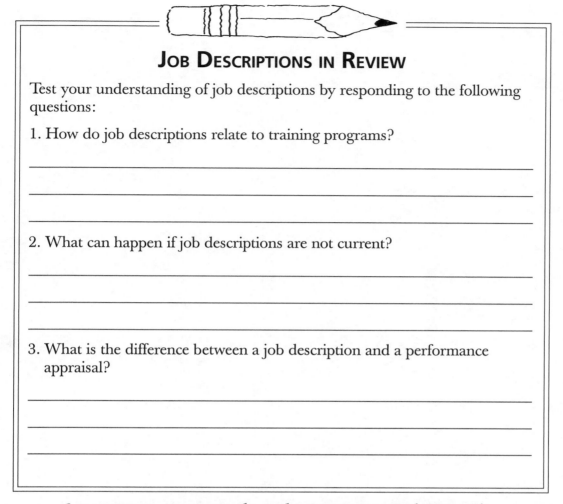

## JOB DESCRIPTIONS IN REVIEW

Test your understanding of job descriptions by responding to the following questions:

1. How do job descriptions relate to training programs?

_____

_____

_____

2. What can happen if job descriptions are not current?

_____

_____

_____

3. What is the difference between a job description and a performance appraisal?

_____

_____

_____

*Compare your answers to the author's responses in the Appendix.*

For more practice in developing job descriptions, turn to the practice activity in the Appendix.

# P A R T 4

# Plan the Training

# The Importance of Planning

Now that you have learned about developing a position analysis, you should know all major aspects of the job to be done. Training based on the position analysis must:

➤ Address all tasks

➤ Teach the correct procedures

➤ Determine the required quality levels

With the position analysis done, it is time to plan the training. Some trainers omit or de-emphasize planning, thinking: "What is there to plan? We do the work every day and should be able to show someone how to do it. Time saved in planning can be spent elsewhere!"

But failure to plan for training activities is a sure way to have your training efforts fail.

To plan for training, a trainer must:

1. Determine training objectives

2. Develop a training plan

3. Design a training lesson

4. Select the trainer(s)

5. Prepare the trainee(s)

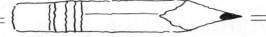

# WHAT CAN HAPPEN IF YOU DON'T PLAN?

Think about training programs in which you have been involved. Some of these programs may be currently used in your organization. Circle the numbers for any of the following mishaps that have occurred.

1. The trainer "forgot" that training was to take place.

2. As a trainee, you were uncertain about what you needed to learn.

3. The training was often interrupted because of outside priorities.

4. The quality of training was lowered by the lack of supplies or unavailable equipment.

5. The procedures taught by the trainer were not consistent with:

   ❏ What the written or audiovisual materials said to do

   ❏ What others told you to do

   ❏ What you saw others do

6. The training was disorganized (for example, procedures were taught out of sequence).

7. The trainer did not seem to care about training you.

8. The trainer was ineffective because of attitude or a lack of knowledge.

9. There were no written (or other) materials to help you learn.

10. Too little time was reserved for training, thus the training was not completed or was rescheduled.

11. The training was done at such a high (or low!) level that the group being trained was not really motivated to learn.

12. Training was done "only when there was time."

If you had first-hand experience with any of the above, you know why planning your training sessions is essential.

# Activity #1: Determine Training Objectives

**Planning for Training:
The Five Activities**

❏ Determine Training Objectives

❏ Develop a Training Plan

❏ Design a Training Lesson

❏ Select the Trainer(s)

❏ Prepare the Trainee(s)

You cannot plan a program until you know what the training is to accomplish. This is where training objectives come into consideration.

This book began with its own objectives: what you, the reader, should know or be able to do after you complete this guide. In the same way, as you plan a training program, you must consider what trainees should know or be able to do after the training is completed.

Training objectives should be *attainable*. If the set goals are impossible to reach, the trainer and the trainees will be frustrated. Objectives also should be *measurable*. At the conclusion of the training program, the trainer and trainees should be able to determine how well the goals were met.

Objectives also come into consideration during the evaluation stage, which will be discussed later. The training program will be judged successful if the objectives are met.

# SETTING GOOD OBJECTIVES

The following sample training objectives will help you understand what makes training program objectives realistic and effective. Mark which of the following objectives are attainable and/or measurable.

|  | Attainable | Measurable |
|---|:---:|:---:|
| 1. There will never be any accidents. | ❏ | ❏ |
| 2. Accident rates can be reduced. | ❏ | ❏ |
| 3. Employees will always have the proper attitude about safety. | ❏ | ❏ |
| 4. Employees can be taught to operate the equipment according to procedures in the task breakdown. | ❏ | ❏ |
| 5. Employees will appreciate the need to operate equipment safely. | ❏ | ❏ |
| 6. Employees can be trained to complete an accident follow-up report correctly. | ❏ | ❏ |
| 7. Employees can be trained to correctly perform each task for their position. | ❏ | ❏ |

*Compare your answers to the author's responses in the Appendix.*

# Activity #2: Develop a Training Plan

> **Planning for Training:**
> **The Five Activities**
>
> ❑ Determine Training Objectives
>
> ❑ Develop a Training Plan
>
> ❑ Design a Training Lesson
>
> ❑ Select the Trainer(s)
>
> ❑ Prepare the Trainee(s)

Once you have determined attainable and measurable training objectives, you can develop a training plan. The plan can be for a complete training program or can focus on just one task. Either way, the training plan provides a step-by-step written document for others to follow.

## Professional Trainer's Tip

Keep an individual training record for each employee. Trainees' progress can be tracked on the computer or you can record the information manually for storage in their personnel files.

# SAMPLE TRAINING PLAN

| Session | Date | Time | Employees Involved | Training Objective | Training Site | Trainer(s) | Equipment or Supplies | Method/ Lesson # |
|---|---|---|---|---|---|---|---|---|
| 1 | 6/8 | 8:00–10:00 | JH/JS | 1, 2 | Lunch-room | Jim | OH proj. | Lecture 1 |
| 2 | 6/15 | 9:00–10:00 | JH/JS | 3, 4 | Sales Office | Jim | VHS/mon. | Individual 2 |
| 3 | 6/22 | 7:30–9:30 | JH/JS | 5, 6 | Sales Office | Jim | Black-board | Lecture 3 |
| 4 | | | | | | | | |
| 10 | 8/12 | 10:00–11:00 | JH/JS | 19, 20 | Client's Office | Jim | None | Individual 10 |

**NOTE:** Training plans outline a broad schedule. General plans are normally designed for several sessions.

# Involving Employees in Training

Much of the information in this book is focused on the trainer. But trainers also should take into account the individuals for whom the training program is being developed.

Indeed, with today's emphasis on quality service, employees are becoming more involved in many aspects of business operation. And there are many ways that trainees can be involved in developing and implementing training programs.

Because of a variety of factors, including age and cultural heritage, however, some workers may be hesitant to "tell the boss" how things should be done. But you will be able to get valuable input from all members of your work group if you are friendly and sincere.

The following list describes ways to involve trainees in developing training programs. Check (✔) any procedures currently used in your program. Also note those that are not currently used, but should be.

| | In Use | Needed |
|---|---|---|
| Employees are surveyed about current training needs. | ❏ | ❏ |
| Employees are interviewed about ways that orientation programs can be improved. | ❏ | ❏ |
| Employees evaluate current training programs and are given an opportunity to comment on how they can be improved. | ❏ | ❏ |
| Training programs maximize participation by trainees. | ❏ | ❏ |
| Trainees evaluate trainers following each program. | ❏ | ❏ |
| Trainees evaluate the training environment following each program. | ❏ | ❏ |
| During performance reviews, employees are asked about the relationship between training activities and job requirements and performance. | ❏ | ❏ |
| Recent trainees are solicited to endorse the need for training with their peers. | ❏ | ❏ |
| Trainees are asked how to improve training during the program itself and not just at the conclusion of training. | ❏ | ❏ |

## Professional Trainer's Tip

When trainees are involved in creating their own training programs, they learn faster and retain the information they have learned better than if they are not involved.

# Choosing Group or Individual Training

An essential decision in planning a training program is whether to use group or individual training. Most successful programs involve some of each. Some on-the-job training is best done in groups.

The following factors should be considered when you are deciding between group and individual training. For each one, check (✔) the type of training that you believe is generally better.

| Situation | Best Training Method | |
|---|---|---|
| | Group | Individual |
| 1. The same information is to be presented to several individuals. | ❑ | ❑ |
| 2. The primary purpose of training is to present a wide range of extensive details. | ❑ | ❑ |
| 3. Time is limited and several trainees must be trained. | ❑ | ❑ |
| 4. The trainees' experience and background are similar. | ❑ | ❑ |
| 5. Cost is a consideration. | ❑ | ❑ |
| 6. Training needs to involve the trainee personally. | ❑ | ❑ |
| 7. Highly specialized training is required. | ❑ | ❑ |
| 8. The trainer doesn't have much time for planning. | ❑ | ❑ |

*Compare your answers with the author's responses in the Appendix.*

# TEST YOUR KNOWLEDGE OF GROUP TRAINING

Check (✔) each of the following statements as either true or false.

|  |  | True | False |
|---|---|:---:|:---:|
| 1. | Group training programs do not require a statement of objectives because each trainee is likely to finish training at a different skill level. | ❏ | ❏ |
| 2. | The results of group training should be evaluated when the training is completed and after trainees return to the job. | ❏ | ❏ |
| 3. | Rehearsing group training activities is unnecessary because spontaneous presentations are best. | ❏ | ❏ |
| 4. | Training presentations are important but the training environment is not. | ❏ | ❏ |
| 5. | If handouts are used, the trainer need not provide an oral overview of the program when it begins. | ❏ | ❏ |
| 6. | If training is being conducted to resolve a problem, both the problem and the results of the solution should be discussed beforehand. | ❏ | ❏ |
| 7. | Participants in group training are less likely to resist change than those given individual training. | ❏ | ❏ |
| 8. | If a trainer is effective, each participant in the group training is likely to react the same way during training. | ❏ | ❏ |
| 9. | Good trainers will adapt their style to the needs of the group. | ❏ | ❏ |
| 10. | It is generally unwise to ask questions of trainees unless a trainer is concerned about "filling" time. | ❏ | ❏ |

*Compare your answers with the author's responses in the Appendix.*

# Activity #3: Design a Training Lesson

**Planning for Training:
The Five Activities**

❑ Determine Training Objectives

❑ Develop a Training Plan

❑ Design a Training Lesson

❑ Select the Trainer(s)

❑ Prepare the Trainee(s)

What exactly does the trainer do during a training session? How much time should be allowed? These are two of the questions answered in a *training lesson,* which concentrates on specific segments of the overall training program. Generally, there is one training lesson for each training session. Thus, if 10 sessions are planned, 10 training lessons are developed.

Having a training lesson accomplishes the following:

➤ It provides a content outline for the session

➤ It suggests activities or specific instructions to facilitate training

➤ It defines time frames for each segment within the session

If the specific training session is designed to teach employees how to perform a task, the task breakdown you defined on page 30 becomes a major part of the training lesson. In this way, an important job-planning tool becomes an important training tool.

# SAMPLE TRAINING LESSON

Training Topic: _Operate company cash register properly_

Objectives(s): _Once training is completed, a sales associate should know how to operate the cash register to company specifications._

| Content of Session | Suggested Activities | Time |
|---|---|---|
| 1. Procedures for cash register operations are found in the operations manual for the machine and augmented by company manuals for special purchases. | 1. Provide a copy of instructions from the manual. | N/A |
| | 2. Talk through the operating techniques. | 10 min. |
| | 3. Use training software; work through several examples of machine operation. | 40 min. |
| | 4. Review what has been learned by allowing trainees to demonstrate their understanding via "real-world" examples. | 10 min. per trainee |

**Note:** The "Content" column may include actual information (such as the task breakdown) or information the instructor has adapted from other resources such as books or magazines. Suggested activities should allow trainees to participate in the training program.

# Collecting Resource Material

As a trainer, you cannot simply sit at your desk to develop training programs. Fortunately, a wide range of resource material is available for you to use to develop and conduct training activities.

Do not wait until a program must be developed to start collecting applicable information. Be on the lookout as you read your business mail or attend trade shows, and begin developing a "library" of materials for all of your applicable training activities. The following are excellent sources:

➤ Manufacturers' operating manuals (for equipment)

➤ A procedures manual for your organization

➤ Task breakdowns for jobs within each department

➤ Applicable magazines for your business

➤ Trade magazines devoted to training, human resource management, and so on

➤ Promotional flyers from training companies

➤ Training programs from nearby educational institutions

➤ Libraries available to you

➤ Industry-specific trade associations

➤ Distributor's representatives selling products, equipment, or supplies that could be useful during training

➤ "Friendly competition" (training ideas gained from those in related businesses)

➤ "Canned" training programs (packaged programs that present generic training information)

➤ Outside consultants who can be hired to teach specific programs to employees

➤ Chambers of commerce and other business-oriented groups

## Professional Trainer's Tip

Spend more of your valuable time delivering training programs and less time developing them by maintaining a "training ideas" file. Include information on training programs you can use "as is," as well as material that could be incorporated into training programs you develop.

# Activity #4: Select the Trainer(s)

**Planning for Training:
The Five Activities**

❏ Determine Training Objectives

❏ Develop a Training Plan

❏ Design a Training Lesson

❏ Select the Trainer(s)

❏ Prepare the Trainee(s)

Who is going to train? If you are a manager, there is a good chance you will conduct the training. Sometimes, however, you may select a fellow manager or even a highly skilled employee to assist you in your training efforts.

Not just anyone would be an effective co-trainer. What should you consider when selecting an individual to help you with employee training? The exercise on the following page will lead you to some clues.

# WHO WOULD MAKE A GOOD CO-TRAINER?

The following list includes possible considerations for choosing your co-trainer. Circle the ones that you think should be taken into account in making your decision.

1. The best trainers will be found in the human resources department.

2. The most experienced employee will automatically be the best trainer.

3. The trainer must have an interest in training.

4. The trainer should have a sense of humor.

5. The trainer must be a good communicator.

6. The trainer must have patience.

7. The trainer must be a manager.

8. The trainer must have the time to train.

9. The trainer must have the respect of colleagues.

10. The trainer must be "higher up" in the organization.

11. The trainer must be enthusiastic.

12. The trainer must be the person who developed the training plan and training lesson.

13. The trainer must personally know how to do every task that is required of someone in the position being trained.

14. The trainer must be interested in the success of each trainee.

15. The trainer must be the same age range as the trainee.

*Compare your answers to the author's responses in the Appendix.*

# Activity #5: Prepare the Trainee(s)

**Planning for Training:**
**The Five Activities**

❏ Determine Training Objectives

❏ Develop a Training Plan

❏ Design a Training Lesson

❏ Select the Trainer(s)

❏ Prepare the Trainee(s)

As a trainer, you must always consider the trainees' individual needs and prepare them for the training. To do so, consider ways to:

➤ Reduce anxieties by telling trainees what the training will involve.

➤ Emphasize that trainee concerns will be addressed.

➤ Inform trainees that training will directly relate to the work they were hired to do.

➤ Indicate that you will work to keep the training enjoyable and worthwhile.

➤ Let trainees know the basis on which they will be evaluated.

# P A R T 5

# Present
# the Training

# Identifying Training Methods

Once work procedures have been defined and the training program has been planned, it is time to present the training to the trainee(s).

There is a wide range of useful training methods. These include:

> **Lectures:** A trainer speaks to the trainees. Videos, overheads, slides, films, and the like can supplement the lecture.

> **Role-playing:** Trainees act out situations after learning basic principles.

> **Case studies:** Trainees read, analyze, and discuss real-life situations.

> **Demonstration:** A trainer (or other party) shows how to do something.

> **Self-study materials:** Trainees read and digest self-paced lessons on the Internet and/or in workbooks such as this one.

All of these training methods can be used for groups and individuals. There are other types of individual training as well. But the most common method—and the one covered at length in this book—is on-the-job training (OJT).

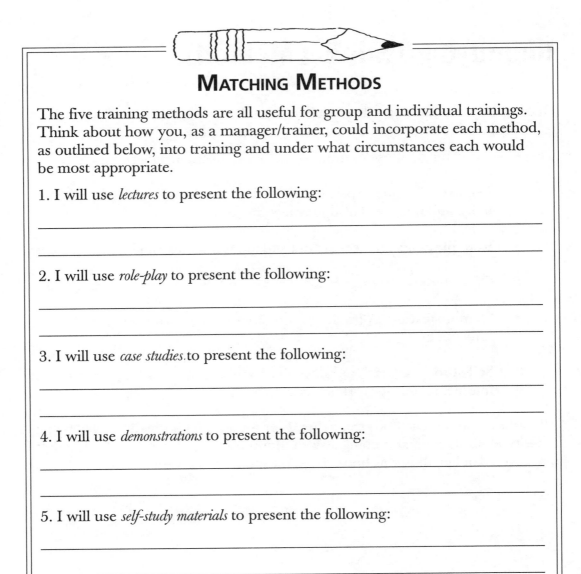

# Matching Methods

The five training methods are all useful for group and individual trainings. Think about how you, as a manager/trainer, could incorporate each method, as outlined below, into training and under what circumstances each would be most appropriate.

1. I will use *lectures* to present the following:

_____

_____

2. I will use *role-play* to present the following:

_____

_____

3. I will use *case studies* to present the following:

_____

_____

4. I will use *demonstrations* to present the following:

_____

_____

5. I will use *self-study materials* to present the following:

_____

_____

## Professional Trainer's Tip

Use the straight lecture style of training sparingly. Most adults learn best when they actively, rather than passively, participate in training. Even when a lecture is the best training method, make sure you allow for questions, participant feedback, and other activities to ensure that your trainees understand and will retain the material you have presented.

# Understanding On-the-Job Training

On-the-job training is the most popular training method for many managers. It is an effective method if done correctly.

Many managers consider OJT the best method because they believe it:

➤ Is simple and fast

➤ Requires no planning

➤ Can be used by anybody

But these beliefs are wrong. These are not the factors that make on-the-job training excellent. In fact:

➤ OJT is simple, but only if considerable planning has been done.

➤ OJT is not fast because you still must take time for planning, delivering, and evaluating the training.

➤ It is a myth that "anybody can train" using this method. The same concerns about trainer selection and the need for preparation apply to OJT as to group training.

Before discussing details of on-the-job training, you must understand that this method can be effective only when basic training principles are used. If they are not, training time will be wasted.

# Making On-the-Job Training Effective

The preceding page presented common myths about OJT. By contrast, the following statements—all true—will tell you what you need to know to make OJT the effective method it can be.

➤ Planning is necessary. Task lists, task breakdowns, performance standards, training plans, and training lessons must be developed before OJT can be used to train new employees.

➤ Trainer selection is important. The trainer must want to train, have adequate job knowledge, and understand and use basic training principles.

➤ Written materials such as task breakdowns, operating procedure manuals, and handbooks can be helpful to reinforce what trainees learn.

➤ Time for training must be provided. It is usually not adequate simply to allow a trainee to "tag along with" or "shadow" a more experienced employee as work is performed.

➤ Before demonstrating a work task, it is essential to prepare the work area, collect all appropriate tools, supplies, and any other necessary items.

➤ Evaluation is an integral part of OJT. This should be considered as you plan the program. Some evaluation is necessary both as the program evolves and at the time of its completion.

➤ Even if a manager delegates OJT to a subordinate, it is important for the manager to "keep up" with training progress. This can be done by interviewing the trainer and trainee and closely observing the trainee as initial work activities are performed.

➤ OJT time should not be squandered teaching tasks an employee already understands. An initial study of the task list along with a demonstration of work required for some tasks can clear the way to emphasize activities with which the trainee is unfamiliar.

# Activity #1: Preparation

> **On-the-Job Training:**
> **The Four Activities**
>
> ❑ Preparation
>
> ❑ Presentation
>
> ❑ Demonstration
>
> ❑ Follow-Up

The first step in on-the-job training–preparation–is the most important and, too often, the most overlooked. Simply stated, a manager does not just "begin training." A wide range of activities must be done to help ensure that training will be successful. Considering the impact that employees have on customers, it is easy to justify careful planning.

The exercise on the next page takes you through each step in OJT. It identifies important training principles and asks you to review an initial training session and improve upon it in the next training opportunity.

Take time to complete the exercises in this section carefully. After completing the worksheet, you will have a greater knowledge about the "mechanics" of developing, implementing, and evaluating an on-the-job training program.

# ON-THE-JOB TRAINING: PREPARATION

Use the following checklist to review and improve your techniques before your next training opportunity. After conducting an initial training session, check (✔) the boxes below to indicate which of these preparation steps you followed. Note the points you do not check and be sure to incorporate these into your next session.

❑ 1. Before training began, you let your employees know what they were to learn and how long the training would last.

❑ 2. You used a written task breakdown.

❑ 3. Before training began, the work area was ready, and all equipment and supplies were present.

❑ 4. You made your employees comfortable before the training began.

❑ 5. Before training began, you gave employees a chance to show that they knew about selected tasks, so you could teach only those activities they didn't already know.

❑ 6. You began each session by telling employees what they were supposed to learn.

❑ 7. You had an effective way to evaluate whether employees had learned each activity.

❑ 8. Once the training session was completed, you consistently observed employees using "the right way."

## Professional Trainer's Tip

When a trainer and a trainee do not share a common primary language, it is still the trainer's responsibility to communicate properly. Using interpreters, learning key words of the trainee's language, and perfecting demonstration methods are all ways that skilled trainers can improve communication with trainees.

# Activity #2: Presentation

**On-the-Job Training:
The Four Activities**

❑ Preparation

❑ Presentation

❑ Demonstration

❑ Follow-Up

Presenting to the trainee should be easy if the trainer is prepared. But this step is not just showing an employee how the work should be done. Instead, the trainer must have adequate time to explain to the trainee what must be done *while* carefully demonstrating the "whats and whys" of each procedure.

Many managers make the mistake of throwing a new employee into the new work setting without any initial training. This is usually not a good technique. Anxiety and stress can make the initial work experiences difficult for a new employee. Product quality and/or customer service can be negatively affected.

Remember that your customers are not paying a reduced price when a trainee serves them. So it is not a good idea to let trainees learn "at the expense" of customers. You must do some training before putting trainees in a position where their output will reach the customer.

# ON-THE-JOB TRAINING: PRESENTATION

Use the following checklist to review and improve your techniques before your next training opportunity. After conducting an initial training session, check (✔) the boxes below to indicate which of these presentation steps you followed. Note the points you do not check and be sure to incorporate these into your next session.

❑ 1. Did you explain each task to employees before you demonstrated it?

❑ 2. Was it apparent to employees that you looked forward to and were enjoying the training?

❑ 3. Did you ask questions and urge employees to ask questions as the initial presentation evolved?

❑ 4. Was each activity organized? Did it follow procedures written in a task breakdown?

❑ 5. Did you give the "right" amount of training in each session? (Could employees have learned more or was too much "crammed" into the time interval?)

❑ 6. Was the training you gave accurate and simple?

❑ 7. Was the training of interest to employees? Were there things that you could have done to make it more interesting?

❑ 8. Could employees tell that you had done effective planning and had experience presenting this phase of the training program?

# Using Visual Aids

You have heard the question many times: "Which came first, the chicken or the egg?" This question can, with revision, be asked as the trainer decides on the role of visual aids in a training program: "Which come first, training program contents or visual training aids?"

We may debate about the first question (the chicken and egg), but there can be no debate about the second. Contents must be determined *before* visual aids can be selected or developed. This may seem obvious, but many trainers get caught up in an excellent topical videotape or CD-ROM and then decide that a training program on this subject would be helpful. It is far better to decide the content first and then determine how to present that content.

The use of a visual aid may be effective, but it is also possible that a role-play, handout, on-the-job demonstration, or other method might be better (and less expensive) than a visual aid.

Determine program content first and then find the best method to present it. Do not use a visual aid unless it is an ideal technique for delivering the training subject matter or it clearly supports the content you are presenting.

## Professional Trainer's Tip

*Immediately before* the training session begins, always check visual aids you will use. Make sure sound levels are appropriate, videotapes and overheads can be seen easily, and computer-displayed presentations are working properly. Nonfunctioning visual aids waste training time and can lead trainees to think the trainer is unprepared and unprofessional.

# Activity #3: Demonstration

> **On-the-Job Training:**
> **The Four Activities**
>
> ❏ Preparation
>
> ❏ Presentation
>
> ❏ Demonstration
>
> ❏ Follow-Up

Demonstration starts with the *trainer* doing the task, and then having the trainees show the trainer what they have learned. The trainer should closely observe trainees and provide immediate feedback—positive reinforcement or corrective action—to help trainees apply what they learned from the demonstration. This is more effective than having the trainee work alone and the trainer returning later to check performance.

By now, you probably have noticed that the recommended approach to on-the-job training makes it different from the OJT you may have experienced. Can you see why the initial statements about OJT (little time required, no preparation needed, "anyone" can train) are myths?

On-the-job training presents a powerful method to teach employees what they need to know, but these results can happen only when the program is designed and implemented correctly.

## Professional Trainer's Tip

Whenever possible, let trainees know the "why" as well as the "how" of work procedures. Trainees will learn faster and retain more if they understand why a work activity is performed in a specific manner and not merely *how* it is performed.

# ON-THE-JOB TRAINING: DEMONSTRATION

Use the following checklist to review and improve your techniques before your next training opportunity. After conducting an initial training session, check (✔) the boxes below to indicate which of these demonstration steps you followed. Note the points you do not check and be sure to incorporate these into your next session.

❑ 1. Did you ask employees to describe each activity as they initially performed it?

❑ 2. Did you have employees demonstrate tasks?

❑ 3. If employees made errors in their demonstrations, did you promptly indicate what they were and explain exactly what was wrong and why it was wrong?

❑ 4. If employees made errors, did you get upset and blame them for the error?

❑ 5. If employees made errors, did you demonstrate the correct way and then allow employees to practice?

❑ 6. Did you congratulate employees when they did the work correctly?

❑ 7. Did you explain how the task you demonstrated was part of your training program?

❑ 8. Did you question employees to assess whether they knew why work was being done in a specified way?

❑ 9. Did employees have opportunities to demonstrate their learning in a situation that would not directly affect customers?

# Activity #4: Follow-Up

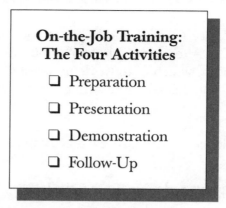

**On-the-Job Training:
The Four Activities**

❑ Preparation

❑ Presentation

❑ Demonstration

❑ Follow-Up

Some managers and trainers omit the follow-up step, thinking it is not necessary if trainees have properly demonstrated what they have learned. But over time, trainees forget the required work procedures. They may discover "shortcuts" that are not better methods than those presented during training. This is why the trainer must follow up and provide corrective action, if necessary, to get trainees "back on track."

Follow-up involves evaluation. Are trainees able to do the work in the correct manner? If the correct procedure is defined (using a task breakdown) and if the correct procedure is taught, the trainer should be able to confirm that training has been successful. Note, however, that the omission of either of these steps—defining or teaching the "correct" method—makes for ineffective training. And the fault will lie with the trainer, not the trainee.

# ON-THE-JOB TRAINING: FOLLOW-UP

Use the following checklist to review and improve your techniques before your next training opportunity. After conducting an initial training session, check (✔) the boxes below to indicate which of these follow-up steps you performed. Note the points you do not check and be sure to incorporate these into your next session.

❑ 1. Did you provide follow-up evaluation?

❑ 2. Did you encourage employees to ask questions after the training was completed?

❑ 3. Did employees know whom to ask for follow-up help, if they needed any?

❑ 4. Did you conduct follow-up observations of employees' work?

❑ 5. Did you encourage employees when you observed them doing the work correctly?

❑ 6. Did you ask employees for ideas about how the job might be improved?

❑ 7. Did you ask employees about ways the training program might be improved?

❑ 8. Did employees feel "good" about the training experience?

❑ 9. Was the training related to the work employees did immediately after training?

❑ 10. Would more or different training have been more effective?

# Evaluate

# the Training

# Principles of Training Evaluation

All trainers need to learn whether their training has been successful. If it has, they can use the subject matter, approach, and training method for additional training efforts. If it has not been successful, current trainees may need additional training, and future programs may need to include different subject matter or use different training methods or techniques.

Moreover, trainees want to know whether they have mastered the material from the training program. Thus, evaluation is important to both trainers and trainees.

Carefully consider the following principles of training evaluation because they will help you more effectively evaluate the success of your training efforts.

1. Evaluation efforts must address the extent to which measurable objectives stated at the beginning of the training are attained.

2. Evaluation must focus on:

   ➤ Training methods

   ➤ Training content

   ➤ Training environment

3. Trainees can be *asked* about training experiences.

4. Trainees can be *observed* to assess training effectiveness.

5. Trainees can be *tested* to measure knowledge gained. (A pre-test about subject matter can be given before the training begins; a post-test made up of questions covering the same material would be given after training is completed.)

6. Trainers must realize that they should use new techniques if training evaluation consistently identifies problems.

7. Evaluation done before the conclusion of training can help a trainer identify areas where changes in training can be helpful.

8. As training programs are planned, trainers should consistently think about how the programs will be evaluated.

9. Training programs should be assessed only after enough time has elapsed to accurately measure the results of the training.

10. Trainers should use results of training evaluation to assess the cost-effectiveness of training efforts.

## Professional Trainer's Tip

Choose the time frame for training program evaluation appropriately. In some cases, it may take weeks or even months to evaluate a training program's true effectiveness. For example, a training session about safe work habits would require a several-month period for tracking any reduction in numbers or severity of workplace injuries or accidents.

# Activity #1: Evaluate by Measuring the Results

> **Training Follow-Up:**
> **The Two Activities**
>
> ❑ Evaluate by Measuring the Results
>
> ❑ Provide Follow-Up Coaching

All managers expect that their training efforts will result in change. If there is no performance change at all, it is fair to ask whether any learning took place. No manager wants to go through the time and effort involved with training without being able to point out areas of improvement. It is not usually enough for workers simply to *know* the new material or method. They must *apply* what they know, and do it on a consistent basis.

Effective training can be expected to make a measurable difference in the following areas:

➤ Attitudes

➤ Values

➤ Knowledge

➤ Skills

## *Whose Job Is It?*

Measuring change is important, but who should be doing it? Sometimes it will be the job of the person conducting the training; sometimes it will not. In your own training situation, think about the answers to the following questions:

1. Who will measure the results of the training?

_____

2. How long should it be until we can see the results of the training?

_____

3. How much change is enough to justify the expense of the training?

_____

4. How accurate are the tools we are using to measure change?

_____

5. How can we tell if the change will be permanent?

_____

# MEASURING THE RESULTS

Every organization has a way to tell whether its employees are performing in an effective and efficient way. For some businesses, it may be how many units are produced per hour or how many guests are served per day. Other businesses may measure the number of telephone calls completed or forms processed.

Now think about your own organization. Can you measure the effect successful training will have on your group? Use the list below to give you ideas for goals to meet as a way to measure your success.

| Impact | Your Goal | | How Much/When? |
|---|---|---|---|
| Decrease | _____ | by | _____ |
| Increase | _____ | by | _____ |
| Reduce | _____ | by | _____ |
| Eliminate | _____ | by | _____ |
| Slow down | _____ | by | _____ |
| Speed up | _____ | by | _____ |
| Create | _____ | by | _____ |
| Stop | _____ | by | _____ |
| Other | _____ | by | _____ |

Using the terms above, or others that fit your organization, complete the sentence below.

I will consider my training program a success, if the change I can measure will

_____our_____
                (impact)                              (goal)

by_____.
                          (how much/when)

# Activity #2: Provide Follow-Up Coaching

> **Training Follow-Up:**
> **The Two Activities**
>
> ❏ Evaluate by Measuring the Results
>
> ❏ Provide Follow-Up Coaching

Is the training program completed once the evaluation has been done? No!

When does training stop and normal supervision begin? This question introduces the concept of coaching.

*Coaching* is the ongoing reinforcement of the positive aspects of training. It involves:

➤ Focusing on special problems that must be resolved

➤ Maintaining open and effective communication with employees

➤ Providing employees with ongoing opportunities for professional growth

Coaching involves communicating with employees about work-related problems. Both the manager and the trainee will engage in a problem-solving process. Relationships should improve, work should be done more effectively, and customers should be better served.

# COACHING PRINCIPLES

Practice the following coaching principles during training sessions you conduct. Circle the numbers for the concepts you already use routinely, and work to incorporate the others into your future decisions.

1. Allow employees to become involved in developing the work procedures they will use.

2. Permit employees to evaluate their work and recommend improvements.

3. Undertake corrective-action interviews in private.

4. Evaluate the work of individual employees by comparing their performance against task breakdowns and job descriptions.

5. Focus on the procedures taught during training–and the way trainees work on the job as the evaluation is done.

6. Establish time frames for corrective action.

7. Have the manager indicate his or her ideas about how work performance can be improved.

8. Establish a schedule for subsequent review of work performance.

9. Allow ample time for "trained" employees to develop skills or build speed.

10. Use open-ended questions to encourage trainees to explain problems they have encountered.

## Professional Trainer's Tip

All employees deserve coaching. When a manager shows inappropriate favoritism to one individual or group, that manager's coaching credibility is diminished.

For more information on this subject, read *Coaching for Development,* by Marianne Minor, Crisp Publications.

# A Final Word

None of the information presented in this book will be of use unless it is applied. As you have worked through this book, your challenge has been to consider how the material could be applied to improve the training activities with which you are involved.

The job of a manager is important. The training responsibilities that you assume as part of that position are significant. You directly affect the lives of your employees and the customers they serve. You have a significant influence on the success of your organization. As a "prepared" trainer, you will gain experiences that will help with your own professional growth.

Best of luck to you in all of your training activities.

# APPENDIX

# Task List

You learned about task lists on page 27. To develop a task list, think about your job. Create a list on the form below for each task you do as part of your job responsibilities. Be complete. Use another sheet of paper if necessary. Ask others who do similar work to analyze your list for additions, deletions, and changes. Ask your manager to do the same. You cannot develop a training program until all tasks for which training is necessary have been defined.

## Task List

Your position: _____

Tasks routinely performed in this position include:

1.

2.

3.

4.

5.

6.

7.

8.

9.

10.

11.

12.

13.

14.

# Task Breakdown

You learned about task breakdowns on page 29. To develop a task breakdown, select a task from your list on the preceding page. Use the form below to explain how it should be done. Use additional paper to continue this analysis if necessary. Share your task breakdown with others who do the same task. Do you agree about the "how, when, and what" of the task? What problems arise when there is no agreement? What are the implications of any disagreement on the design and conduct of future training programs?

## Task Breakdown

| Position: _____ | | Task: _____ | |
|---|---|---|---|
| Step | Process | Equipment/Supplies | Other |
| | | | |

# Job Description

You learned about job descriptions on page 34. Complete the following form for your job. Show it to your supervisor or manager. What differences of opinion, if any, exist about what your job involves? How can this affect your job performance?

## Job Description

Position: _____

Date of last revision: _____

1.  I report to:_____

2.  I supervise: _____

3.  Basic tasks that are part of this position are:

     a. _____

     b. _____

     c. _____

     d. _____

     e. _____

     f. _____

     g. _____

     h. _____

4.  Equipment that I use includes:_____

     _____

5.  Personal qualifications important for this job include: _____

     _____

6.  Other important aspects of this position are:_____

     _____

_____

*This form may be reproduced without further permission.*

# Training Plan

Use the format below, or modify it as needed, to "sketch" a training program you are planning or that your organization conducts.

| Session # | Date | Time | Employees Scheduled | Training Objectives | Training Site | Trainer(s) | Equipment/ Supplies | Instructional Method |
|-----------|------|------|---------------------|---------------------|---------------|------------|---------------------|----------------------|
|           |      |      |                     |                     |               |            |                     |                      |
|           |      |      |                     |                     |               |            |                     |                      |

*This form may be reproduced without further permission.*

# Training Lesson

You learned about training lessons on page 51. Use the format below to develop a training lesson for one task that you regularly do as part of your job.

**Note:** You may want to select the task for which you developed a task breakdown.

## Training Lesson

| Training Topic:_____ |||
|---|---|---|
| Training Objective(s):_____ |||
| Content of Session | Suggested Activities | Estimated Time Required |
|  |  |  |

*This form may be reproduced without further permission.*

# Author's Responses to Exercises

## Take the Training Test (page 22)

1. **True.** Training is difficult for many people. It takes a special effort to define how jobs should be done, and it takes skillful planning to implement the subsequent training. Another reason training can be difficult is that a trainer must have knowledge and skills that go beyond "common sense" and on-the-job experience.

2. **True.** Training must be cost-effective or it should not be undertaken.

3. **True.** Line managers—not those in human resources—ultimately should be responsible for training.

4. **False.** All employees benefit from training.

5. **Maybe.** It is difficult to modify attitudes.

6. **True.** Training typically is most helpful for influencing knowledge and skill levels.

7. **False.** Training is too important to do only when time permits; it must be a priority.

8. **False.** The basic training techniques are the same regardless of the purpose.

## Job Descriptions in Review (page 37)

1. Job descriptions specify tasks for which training is necessary. They also help ensure that qualified employees are hired.

2. Problems will occur when job descriptions do not accurately describe the work that needs to be done.

3. Job descriptions describe tasks that are part of a position. Performance appraisals are methods used by management to evaluate how well a job is being performed.

## Setting Good Objectives (page 44)

1. This is probably not attainable but is measurable. Accidents can be reduced but not eliminated (due to the human factor).

2. This is probably attainable and can be measured by determining if the rate after training is lower than the rate before training.

3. Attitudes are difficult to "measure." This is probably not an attainable objective.

4. This is attainable and measurable.

5. Same answer as #3.

6. This is attainable and measurable. The definition of "correctly" refers to procedures outlined in the job breakdown for each task.

7. Both attainable and measurable.

## Choosing Group or Individual Training (page 49)

Group: 1, 3, 4, 5

Individual: 2, 6, 7

The correct answer for #8 is *neither*. Both methods require extensive planning.

## Test Your Knowledge of Group Training (page 50)

Statements 2, 6, and 9 are true; all other answers are false.

## Who Would Make a Good Co-Trainer? (page 55)

The following characteristics are important in a co-trainer: 3, 4, 5, 6, 8, 9, 11, and 14. *Note:* Statement 13 is not necessary because different co-trainers could teach employees different tasks.

# Recommended Reading

Blanchard, Ken, and Don Shula. *Everyone's a Coach.* Grand Rapids, MI: Zondervan Publishing House, 1996.

Blanchard, Ken, and Sheldon Bowles. *Gung Ho! Turn on the People in Any Organization.* New York: William Morrow & Co., 1997.

Craig, Robert L. *The ASTD Training and Development Handbook: A Guide to Human Resource Development.* New York: McGraw-Hill Companies, 1996.

Kirkpatrick, Donald. *Evaluating Training Programs: The Four Levels.* San Francisco: Berrett-Koehler, 1998.

Lancaster, Lynne, and David Stillman. *When Generations Collide: Who They Are, Why They Clash, How to Solve the Generational Puzzle at Work.* New York: HarperCollins, 2003.

Lebo, Fern. *Mastering the Diversity Challenge: Easy On-the-Job Applications for Measurable Results.* Boca Raton, FL: CRC Press, 1996.

Maxwell, John C. *Developing the Leader Within You.* Nashville, TN: Thomas Nelson, 2001.

McArdle, Geri. *Delivering Effective Training Sessions: Techniques for Productivity.* Boston, MA: Thomson Learning/Course Technology, 1994.

Rosenberg, Marc. *E-Learning Strategies for Delivering Knowledge in the Digital Age.* New York: McGraw-Hill Companies, 2000.

Scott, Cynthia. *Managing Change at Work: Leading People Through Organizational Transitions.* Boston, MA: Thomson Learning/Course Technology, 1995.

Tamblyn, Doni, and Sharyn Weiss. *The Big Book of Humorous Training Games.* New York: McGraw-Hill Companies, 2000.

Van Daele, Carrie. *50 One-Minute Tips for Trainers: A Quick and Easy Guide.* Boston, MA: Thomson Learning/Course Technology, 1996.

Zemke, Ron, Claire Raines, and Bob Filipczak. *Generations at Work: Managing the Clash of Veterans, Boomers, Xers, and Nexters in Your Workplace.* New York: AMACOM, 2000.

# Now Available From

## THOMSON
## COURSE TECHNOLOGY
™

## Books•Videos•CD-ROMs•Computer-Based Training Products

If you enjoyed this book, we have great news for you. There are over 200 books available in the *Crisp Fifty-Minute™ Series*. For more information contact

**Course Technology**
25 Thomson Place
Boston, MA 02210
1-800-442-7477
www.courseilt.com

## Subject Areas Include:

*Management*
*Human Resources*
*Communication Skills*
*Personal Development*
*Sales/Marketing*
*Finance*
*Coaching and Mentoring*
*Customer Service/Quality*
*Small Business and Entrepreneurship*
*Training*
*Life Planning*
*Writing*